THE LAW OF DIMINISHING RETURNS:

Understand the fundamentals of economic productivity

Written by Pierre Pichère
In collaboration with Brigitte Feys
Translated by Carly Probert

THE LAW OF DIMINISHING RETURNS

KEY POINTS

- **Names:** Law of diminishing returns, law of variable pro-portions, principle of diminishing marginal productivity, diminishing marginal returns
- **Uses:** Business economics, sectorial economy, theories of innovation, studies on the creation of rent
- **Why is it successful?** As a short-term theory, it promotes the best decisions on the allocation of production factors
- **Key words:**
  - <u>Average</u>: The result of adding all of the elements in a series, then dividing the result by the number of units that make it up.
  - <u>Capital</u>: A factor of production including everything outside of human labor (machines, bank assets, etc.).
  - <u>Economy of scale</u>: The phenomenon that leads to lower costs as the quantity produced increases, due to the amortization of initial investments.
  - <u>Margin</u>: The difference between the cost price and the selling price.
  - <u>Returns</u>: Ratio between the result obtained from a task and the allocated time.
  - <u>Rent</u>: Income from holding capital or, according to the Ricardian analysis, the income of the holders of the first units put into production when the performance of the last units begins to decrease.
  - <u>Work</u>: Human activity carried out in exchange for compensation.

INTRODUCTION

By taking elements from the thinking of economists from the eighteenth century, who focused on the issues facing agricultural production, David Ricardo (British economist, 1772-1823) created the theory of diminishing returns. This is still relevant today thanks to the developments that economics has added to the original formula.

History

Illustrated by David Ricardo in *On the Principles of Political Economy and Taxation* (1817), the theory of diminishing returns is the outcome of this thinking, firstly by the Anglican minister and economics professor Thomas Malthus (1766-1834) and secondly by the Physiocrats, especially Anne Robert Jacques Turgot (French statesman and economist, 1727-1781). Malthus argued that a rising population leads to a reduction of available resources, while Turgot pointed out that any increase in the area of cultivated land would inevitably lead to lower returns, with the best land being exploited first.

EXTRA INFORMATION

The work of the school of Physiocrats (from the Greek 'phusis' meaning 'nature' and 'kratein' meaning 'to govern') on the creation of economic wealth, particularly distribution, is considered revolutionary for its time.

David Ricardo extends and develops this thinking which has become a classic in economics and one of the most famous controversies. Another great economist of the time, Scotsman Adam Smith (1723-1790), developed a contrasting theory on increasing returns from improved productivity, gained through the specialization of tasks.

Definition of the model

David Ricardo, inspired by the economists of the eighteenth century, identifies three factors of production: land (considered the only true value-creating element at the time), capital and labor. He takes the example of the earth to explain the phenomenon of diminishing returns: the more a farmer grows his land, the less the revenue will be for each new plot (marginal revenue, i.e. the revenue of the new plot compared to the previous plots), as the better land will be cultivated first. Further labor is then required to farm the land. Therefore, the total land rent (income received by the owner thereof) will actually increase with the number of plots, but not linearly, as the returns will decrease.

The model has found applications beyond agriculture. In general, the law of diminishing returns describes how the performance of an additional unit of a factor of production, all things being equal, will be less than the return of the units of the same factors previously used in production.

THEORY – THE CONCEPT

Considered to be one of the most influential economists of the classical school alongside Adam Smith and Thomas Malthus, David Ricardo wrote many theories including the exchange value of a product, the opposition to protectionism, the concept of comparative advantage and even the reference to the gold standard for the production of money and, finally, the theory detailed here: the law of rent. In his approach to economics, David Ricardo does not seek moral conformity, unlike Adam Smith and, especially, Thomas Malthus. The latter, a pastor, focused more on the world that men should create to achieve the divine plan, rather than on society as it was at the time.

DAVID RICARDO

David Ricardo was first interested in the mechanism of creating wealth and distribution. To understand the law of diminishing returns, we must remember that reference is made to marginal returns, i.e. the returns of a new unit put into production according to previous units. Moreover, this law applies only when there is variation of one factor of production. During the economist's time, the 'work' and 'capital' factors were not so easily identified. The classical school considered that there was work behind capital, some – Adam Smith, David Ricardo and Karl Marx (socialism theorist and German revolutionary, 1818-1883) in particular – distinguished between productive labor and unproductive labor. The work is called 'productive' when it creates value, but all work does not systematically create value.

Take Ricardo's example of farmland, which allowed him to introduce the concept of 'incorporated work' (the addition of the worker's work and the work required to produce the machines and tools he will use) and consider that there are two factors of production: the land and a composite assembly of labor and capital.

- **Decreasing intensive margin.** Let's apply a greater amount of capital/labor to this land. It will mobilize more labor and prompt the salary budget to rise. The total production costs will thus inevitably increase, lowering the marginal returns: the new production units assigned to work on the land will yield less than the previous units. The intensive margin of crops (i.e. the accelerated exploitation of land) is decreasing.
- **Decreasing extensive margin.** Imagine now that the new land is cultivated, without variation of capital/labor. Again, even without an increase in the amount of work per square meter of land, new workers will be hired. Ricardo, following in the footsteps of the Physiocrats, says, firstly, that the best land is often cultivated first and, on the other hand, all this leads to a return from the new area being cultivated that is lower than the old. The extensive margin of cultivation is also decreasing. Incidentally, for the holder of the most productive areas, there is the creation of rent, a central phenomenon in the Ricardian thought. Already valued by the Physiocrats and Adam Smith as the fruit of the abundant fertility of the land, it comes from Ricardo that there is a scarcity of good land and therefore constitutes an advantage for the owner of the best land without merit or work.

Therefore, the intensive margin and the extensive margin are correlated. In fact, a farmer will gradually increase the use of his land. Then, when the performance of this production unit has decreased too much, he will cultivate new land. Their initial performance will certainly be lower than that of the first, and will also decrease in any case. The amount of useable land is limited; the performance of agriculture is therefore progressively declining. In addition, population growth, by leading to reduced resources and reduced national productivity, generates lower returns that could cripple the country's economy.

This is where innovation comes in – in the agricultural process, this could be machinery or products, such as fertilizers or GMOs, which are controversial today – which will boost the efficiency of the land, lowering costs to counteract the natural tendency of diminishing returns. It is therefore essential, according to David Ricardo, to not only promote technological progress to increase yields according to demand, but to also specialize in an area of activity which is the most productive (see the theory of comparative advantage also developed by the economist).

EXTRA INFORMATION: THE COMPARATIVE ADVANTAGE

A defender of free trade, David Ricardo formalized the theory of comparative advantage. In a closed economy situation, each country should produce what it needs, due to the trade barriers that make imports excessively costly. If the economy opens up to international trade, then each state can produce the goods for which is has a comparative advantage (e.g. a more skilled workforce, a more modern production system, more favorable soil or climate in the case of agricultural products) and import the products is has chosen not to produce, because other countries are better at production or offer a lower price. This theory is now the basis of the thoughts on the proponents of free trade, including the World Trade Organization (WTO).

Theorists would have thought that the law of diminishing returns applied only to agriculture. Ricardo would have been more of a master of agronomy than an economist. Yet in his work, agriculture is just one example, as David Ricardo formulates a universal law of economics, applicable to any industry.

ALFRED MARSHALL

Alfred Marshall (British economist, 1842-1924) shows that this law not only applies to the agricultural economy. He also relates to another holding of the earth: construction. The most developable land (far away from rivers, not prone to flooding, stable, with a nice view, etc.) is used first. Less favorable land is then used for building.

Finally, Alfred Marshall seeks to apply the law of diminishing returns to all industry sectors. For example, imagine a production company with three printing presses. To improve its profit, the company increases it cadences, the workers do more work, etc. But these changes create a constant increase in costs that ultimately makes the acquisition of a fourth machine more cost-effective. The overall labor costs have increased – nowadays we are no longer in the age of automation or offshoring – the marginal profitability of the fourth press will certainly be lower than the first three. Marshall uses the term 'almost-rent' to refer to the income of the first machines; the mechanism is similar to that of ground rent in Ricardo's theory. As we will see below, Marshall included this reflection on the diminishing returns in industry in a broader sequencing: proportional returns allow him to articulate a growth phase and a phase of diminishing returns. There is therefore an inflection point, where the acquisition of an additional unit not only causes an increase, but also a decrease in productivity.

Increasing and diminishing returns

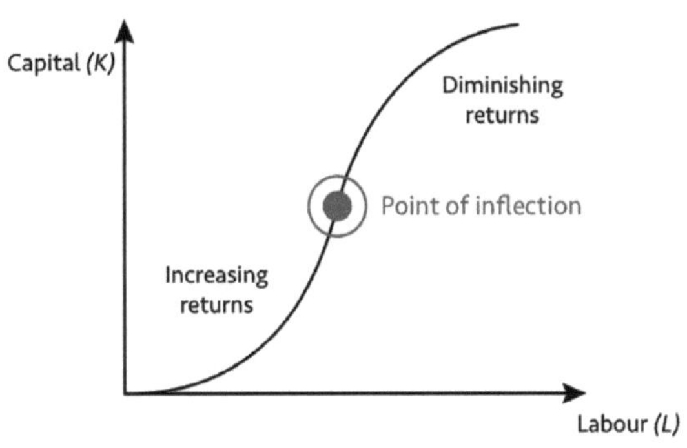

DIMINISHING RETURNS TODAY

Nowadays, land is no longer considered to be a factor of production, but work and capital have been differentiated further than they were in David Ricardo and Adam Smith's time. The law of diminishing returns is still understood today: for a given level of productivity of production factors, the increase of one of these factors (work or capital) will only lead to an increase in productivity that is weaker and weaker.

LIMITS AND EXTENSIONS OF THE MODEL

A theory founded upon classical economics, the law of diminishing returns has attracted much criticism, but also useful developments to enrich the analysis.

LIMITS AND CRITICISMS OF THE MODEL

With the law of diminishing returns, David Ricardo seems to take the opposite view of Adam Smith. The latter, in his book *An Inquiry into the Nature and Causes of the Wealth of Nations* (1776), actually offers a theory of increasing returns. Inspired by the British economist Richard Cantillon (1680-1734) and Pierre Le Pesant de Boisguilbert (Frenchman, 1646-1714), Adam Smith argued that the division of labor leads to an increase in productivity – also called 'economies of scale' – which constantly improves returns. The most famous example developed by the economist is the pin factory. By specializing workers in 18 jobs, each produced 4 800 pins a day, whereas if each employee was performing all the tasks in the production process, he would not make more than 20 pins a day! The division of labor increases the ability of each worker, saves time and drives the invention of new machines and the emergence of entire economic sectors (for example, business services, robotics or logistics in our modern economy).

The opposition between Adam Smith and David Ricardo on this point, however, seems to be bypassed because Ricardo's model does not prohibit the division of labor as it exposes a work dynamic in a given context. Thus, once the work of manufacturing pins is divided into 18 jobs, adding new employees into the factory would lead to a decrease in marginal returns. Only the invention of a new machine or additional division of labor will be able to make returns grow again. This was perfectly observed by Alfred Marshall, who developed the theory of inhomogeneous returns. After an initial growth thanks to technical progress and the division of labor, they will then decrease, which is coherent with the predictions of David Ricardo.

Karl Marx, an avid reader of David Ricardo, created a law called the 'tendency of the rate of profit to fall' (TRPF), based on that of diminishing returns. He highlights that in a context of heightened competition between capitalist enterprises, the profitability rate tends to fall inexorably. The theory of diminishing returns is therefore used in a radical critique of capitalism that alienates humans for its benefit and, for this reason, is denounced by the defenders of the capitalist systems. This hypothesis for the falling rate of profit would be denied by the capacity for innovation continually shown by economic actors. But this attributes intentions to Ricardo that are far from his own, since he had not formulated his theory to criticize a system of organization, but to describe a phenomenon at work in production.

Many economists now believe that diminishing returns is an interesting model for the short term in a given productive environment. Managerial or technological innovation can fortunately overcome this stage of diminishing returns to regain increasing returns. However, this forces entrepreneurs to always push the boundaries of what they know, or risk seeing their performance gradually collapse.

EXTENSIONS AND RELATED MODELS

Returns to scale

The model of diminishing marginal returns only applies to the variation of production factors. The economic theory, under the leadership of Alfred Marshall, is also interested in the variation of all factors of production: which is called returns to scale, which reflects the search for efficiency (doing more with less) following an increase in production factors.

- Returns are increased as long as the percentage of additional earnings (y) exceeds the percentage of costs incurred by the rise of two factors (x). The growth size of the company will lead to better technique and working conditions will certainly attract the most skilled workers: $y > x$
- Returns will begin to decrease with the company effects linked to internal organization (e.g. growing volume of staff). Large companies are more difficult to run than small companies: management and communication become increasingly complex, the objectives of the big business are far from those of its workers that are diluted in multiple divisions, often geographically far away, and management is also perceived as more distant, especially if the company is bought by an international group or holding: $y < x$

This theory enables you to optimize the size of the business and maximize performance: increasing returns ($y > x$) for small quantities (as long as capacities are not saturated) to become constant ($y = x$), and diminishing returns ($y < x$) for very large quantities. Stagnation is then observed as well as saturation (too fast a pace, storage problems, etc.). These problems will result, over time, in return reductions.

The isoquants

Another related model is the isoquants (curves) in microeconomics, studied by Charles Cobb (American mathematician, 1875-1949) and Paul Douglas (American economist, 1892-1976). This describes, for a given volume of factors, all optimal combinations that will produce the highest return for a given level of production. By analyzing the relationship between factors of production – the amount of work and capital – Charles Cobb and Paul Douglas seek to demonstrate that they are substitutable.

Their production function, also called the Cobb-Douglas function, will be as follows: $Y = c.K^{\alpha}.L^{\beta}$ where Y represents the level of production, K represents capital, L represents labor and c, α and β represent the variations linked to technology.

APPLICATIONS

Thus, microeconomics and business economics, which apply to the management of knowledge gained from economics, have long demonstrated a keen enthusiasm for the theory of diminishing returns, as formulated by David Ricardo and developed by Alfred Marshall.

The theory of diminishing returns is of great interest for a business leader. If he maintains one of the production factors and develops a second, it allows him to determine:

- up to what point he will make money;
- from what point the cost of the additional unit, also known as the 'marginal', will exceed the earnings it generates.

INCREASING RETURNS TO START, FOLLOWED BY DIMINISHING RETURNS

To fully understand the model, it is important to remember the contributions of Alfred Marshall: when a production factor varies, returns begin to grow. Then, slowly, as the factor continues to increase, the returns will grow less quickly to the point of balance, before decreasing.

To illustrate this phenomenon, we can look at the example of the pin factory used by Adam Smith. Until the maximum rates are reached, adding additional workers will increase returns. For example, creating a night shift will not affect the return – this more intensive use of the machine will only reduce the life of the machine. But when mass recruitment leads to an increase in labor costs, each team does not work as well because of the presence of others or there is a malfunction/overcrowding of the organization, returns will diminish.

What factor varies?

In the most commonly selected examples, those of companies with industrial machines, it is the work that is chosen as the variable factor, the cost of an additional hour of work is less than that of acquiring a machine. However, they are also of companies offering services, such as counseling, and more generally in contemporary Western economies where labor costs are high due to the necessary financing of social protection. Modern machines, like computers or robots, have very low costs today, so that companies tend to vary in the first capital input, without adding an employee, when the marginal return on capital starts to decrease. This inclination is probably enhanced by the protection of workers, making the work factor less mobile than capital. It also defends the logic of pure productivity: by cons, if we take the 'basic skills' aspect (management skills, corporate social responsibility), we would end up with all other perspectives…which could perhaps be the salvation of our savings!

Margin and average

In order to apply the principle of diminishing returns, it is necessary to recall the fundamental difference between the average productivity and the marginal productivity:

- the average productivity means the returns of all units of the production factors studied. It does not therefore only refer to the opportunity to add an additional unit of one factor or the other;
- the marginal productivity, in turn, precisely indicates the surplus provided by the addition of this unit.

This clarification is important, as the average productivity may continue to increase as the marginal productivity begins to decrease. Thus, imagine that a supermarket calculates the number of customers that pass through the checkout in one hour. The first checkout welcomes ten customers per hour, and then the second welcomes twelve customers, while the first checkout continues to welcome ten. The marginal returns of the second checkout are increasing, since it is higher than the first. The average productivity has also increased: an average of ten customers seen by one checkout rises to an average of eleven with two checkouts.

Encouraged by this good result, the store gets to work and opens a third checkout. The first two continue to receive the same number of customers, but the third only receives eleven in one hour. The average productivity of three checkouts remains unchanged from the situation with two: eleven customers per hour. However, the marginal productivity of the third checkout has decreased compared to the previous checkout. This factor is not enough to positively evolve the returns of the checkouts. The average, however, does not show this.

Marginal revenue and marginal cost

To understand the application of diminishing returns in business activities, two concepts need to be introduced:

- marginal revenue (MR) is generated by the changing factor, corresponding to the revenue share attributable only to the new unit of the added factor in the company production;
- marginal cost (MC) is the cost of acquisition of a new unit of a variable factor.

As long as marginal revenue is greater than the marginal costs, the company will make money, although the gains are lower due to the decrease in the overall returns: MR / DM = return.

At the right time

Microeconomics offers, from the model established by David Ricardo, the calculations determining up to what point the returns of a production factor will increase. This allows for the evaluation of the optimal amount of labor or capital to invest to maximize returns.

This step is crucial for businesses because there is no point over-investing: using the initial phase of return growth allows for investment at the right time, just before the factor concerned begins the inevitable decline in performance.

CASE STUDY – THE OIL INDUSTRY

One of the most telling examples of diminishing returns comes from the oil industry. This sector is the subject of extensive studies and a specialization of some economists, since oil, as the raw material, is vital for the entire global economic system. We also illustrate here the logic of the theory of David Ricardo and Alfred Marshall through a recent topical issue. Note that oil has a particular characteristic: it is a non-renewable raw material. The reasoning here is therefore slightly different from what David Ricardo holds for land, since it regenerates (under the right conditions) its ability to grow plants. In the case of oil, as is the case with coal, deposits will eventually run out.

From the first well to the conventional limits

The first oil well, in the mid-nineteenth century, reached a depth of 28 meters. Currently, the ongoing projects, surrounding oceanic deposits of shale oil, are several thousands of meters deep. This race for depth is the industrial response to the logic of diminishing returns.

Until the mid-nineties, it was estimated that it was impossible to exploit a number of deposits, including those located in deep waters. But the best known, so-called 'conventional' oil deposits, i.e. those located within a reasonable depth and of a sufficient quality to require no treatment other than refining, ended up being exploited. We then stood at the edge of increasing returns, most likely in some sort of equilibrium before the fall. In fact, at that time, adding capital (drilling machines) to increase the depth of research would result in a cost increase as the marginal return would have immediately decreased. Incidentally, the most abundant deposits, exploited long before, formed rent in the form of new deposits, which were less productive, and were put into operation. We will shortly see how rent is formed according to David Ricardo.

Technological innovation

Among the factors that allowed these new operations, there is of course technological innovation. Advances in drilling techniques have allowed oil companies to limit the costs for additional research. Similarly, in the case of oil sands that operate primarily in Canada, the separation technology for oil and other minerals has changed dramatically, favoring exploitation that was previously impossible. As we have seen in the theoretical explanation of the model, progress in the production process pushes back the time when the marginal return will stop growing. Note that the innovation cycle is also not complete. Companies are now looking for new processes to exploit deposits deep in the seabed, including in the North Sea.

Marginal prices, overall price and creation of rent

The cards have also been reshuffled by the disruption in the price system. In 1946, the cost was $17.92 per barrel (the price level in constant dollars relative to the base year 2010, on the New York market, NYMEX). In 1995, it stood at $23.96, an increase of just over 30% in 50 years – let's also remember that two oil crises in 1973 and 1979 led to a spike in prices, although this was relatively short. In 1996, oil prices began a gradual descent that, for the time, was still not a sustainable descent, despite some volatility. In 2011, the average price per barrel was $95, a level at which it has more or less remained ever since, apart from some occasional peaks. In 2013, it was around $103.

An increase in demand is, of course, the origin of this price rise. The late nineties mark the acceleration of globalization and the rise of the BRIC (Brazil, Russia, India and China), emerging as immense economic powers. But to illustrate the diminishing returns and the rent that goes with it, it is necessary to understand the mechanism of price formation. The pressure of the demand has facilitated the exploitation of previously inaccessible hydrocarbons, called 'unconventional oil'. Also, the unit cost for the producer of the new exploited oil barrel is greater than for oil derived from the original simple drilling.

Suppose, to simplify the argument, that traditional oil production costs the exploiter 1 and will be sold for 2. In view of the new technological challenges, unconventional oil costs 1.5. To maintain an equivalent margin, the oil company will now offer its product for 3, no longer for 2. But who is going to pay 3 for a product he can acquire for 2? In a hypercompetitive market with oversupply, the producer who sells his product for 3 will not manage to establish himself. But the oil market, far from being perfectly competitive, is influenced by some very powerful economic agents such as OPEC (Organization of the Petroleum Exporting Companies), for example. Neither the country nor the companies engage in a price war. Therefore, if the new fields are more expensive to operate, it is the entire production that will see its price rise. The former producers with lower costs will align with the selling prices of new entrants. This partly explains the sharp rise in oil prices observed over the last 20 years. Moreover, there is the creation of rent, as former producers derive a profit surplus from the new situation, linked to the price difference between conventional and new oil.

Through this example, we can see that the theory of David Ricardo and Alfred Marshall on diminishing returns and the creation of rent remains relevant to explain contemporary economic phenomena.

SUMMARY

- The law of diminishing returns is based on evidence: in the beginning, efforts are carried out in the most productive and therefore more profitable areas; other resources are then exploited if demand exceeds the initial resources.
- The logic is purely mechanistic: after an initial growth phase, changing a factor of production sees short-term stagnation of returns before a decline if nothing is changed in terms of management.
- This economic law, formulated by David Ricardo using the example of agriculture, has been developed and extended to all economic sectors by Alfred Marshall.
- The basic assumption described here is the marginal return, corresponding to the performance of an additional unit of a production factor.
- The diminishing marginal returns lead to the formation of rent for the owners of the first units put into production, which are more profitable than the last.
- Diminishing returns do not condemn the economy to decline, but encourages entrepreneurs to innovate – in products, processes, patterns of organizations, etc. – to maintain their productivity or increase their efficiency and thus their performance.

We want to hear from you!
Leave a comment on your online library
and share your favourite books on social media!

FURTHER READING

BIBLIOGRAPHY

- AREHN. (2005) Le pétrole. [Online]. [Accessed 12 March 2014]. Available from: <http://www.arehn.asso.fr/dossiers/petrole/petrole.html>
- Chaize, T. (No date) Coût de production, coût marginal et prix du pétrole. *Dr Thomas Chaize. Energy & Mining.* [Online]. [Accessed 12 March 2014]. Available from: <http://www.dani2989.com/matiere1/marginalcostoil0212fr.html>
- Jessua, C. (1991) *Histoire de la théorie économique.* Paris: PUF.
- Mansfield, E. (2002) *Économie managériale. Théorie et applications.* Paris: De Boeck.

50MINUTES.com
History
Business
Coaching
EL DIAGRAMA DE ISHIKAWA
LA GUERRA DE PALESTINA DE 1948
DOMINA EL ARTE DEL NETWORKING
IMPROVE YOUR GENERAL KNOWLEDGE
IN A BLINK OF AN EYE !
www.50minutes.com